Rediscovering
the Book of Faith

Open Scripture.
Join the Conversation.
A gift to you from Zion Lutheran Church
www.zionchurchmpls.org
Fall Kickoff—September 13, 2009

AUGSBURG FORTRESS

MINNEAPOLIS

REDISCOVERING THE BOOK OF FAITH

Book of Faith is an initiative of the
Evangelical Lutheran Church in America
God's work. Our hands.

ISBN: 978-0-8066-8065-1
Writers: Mark D. Johns, Philip Quanbeck II, Darin Wiebe
Editor: Bethany Schneck Stolle
Cover design: Spunk Design Machine, spkdm.com
Interior design: Ivy Palmer Skrade

This book was typeset using Sabon and Formata.

The paper used in this publication meets the minimum requirements of
American national Standard for Information Sciences—Permanence of Paper
for Printed Library Materials, ANSI Z329.48-1984.

Manufactured in the U.S.A.
12   11   10   09   08   2   3   4   5   6   7   8   9   10

Contents

1   ABOUT THE BOOK OF FAITH INITIATIVE

3   ABOUT THIS COURSE
      MEMBER ROLES AND RESPONSIBILITIES
      COVENANT

9   SESSION 1
      REDISCOVERING THE FAMILY ALBUM OF GOD'S PEOPLE

19   SESSION 2
      REDISCOVERING THE GOOD NEWS OF JESUS

31   SESSION 3
      REDISCOVERING GOD'S GIFT OF GRACE

About the Book of Faith Initiative

Welcome to the Book of Faith! The Book of Faith initiative invites the whole church to become more fluent in the first language of faith, the language of Scripture, in order that we might live into our calling as a people renewed, enlivened, empowered, and sent by the Word. Book of Faith is an initiative of the Evangelical Lutheran Church in America.

THE BIBLE IS A BOOK OF FAITH

The Bible is the written Word of God that creates and nurtures faith through the work of the Holy Spirit and points us to Christ, the incarnate Word and center of our faith. The Bible invites us into a relationship with God, making demands on our lives and promising us life in Christ. The Bible tells the stories of people living their faith over the centuries and, through its demands and promises, forms us as a people of faith.

THE LANGUAGE OF SCRIPTURE IS OUR FIRST LANGUAGE OF FAITH

The language of the Bible becomes our language. It shapes how we think and speak about God, about the world, and about ourselves. We become renewed, enlivened, and empowered as the language of Scripture forms our hearts, our minds, our community conversation, and our commitments.

WE HAVE A CALLING AS THE PEOPLE OF GOD

Part of our calling is to know, hear, share, and be rooted in Scripture. We are renewed, enlivened, empowered, and sent by the Word. As we live into our calling as people who are formed by Scripture, we become renewed in our faith, enlivened through the Spirit, and empowered through the cross of Christ to serve God and neighbor.

To learn more about the initiative, visit bookoffaith.org

About This Course

WELCOME TO *REDISCOVERING THE BOOK OF FAITH*!

This three-session study explores how the Bible came to be our Book of Faith and what it means for our lives today. You will learn how, why, when, and where the Old and New Testaments were created, explore how the Bible was put together, and examine the impact of the Reformation on our encounter with scripture.

EACH SESSION HAS FOUR SECTIONS:

GATHER
Begin the conversation around the session theme by discussing questions with the members of your group. Learn more about yourself and each other.

STUDY
Watch the session video with your group. Write down your questions, comments, and "Aha" moments, then spend time exploring them as you dig into the Bible together.

SHARE
Reflect on your own life relative to the session theme. Share stories, questions, comments, and new insights with the members of your group.

SEND

From a list of options, choose an activity that will help you integrate new information in ways that are just right for you!

Blessings on your journey.

MEMBER ROLES and RESPONSIBILITIES

LEADER

The leader invites group members to attend and makes arrangements for the sessions. The leader also acts as host, chooses what to do for each session, prepares session material, and guides the group in its conversations.

CHILD CARE COORDINATOR

The child care coordinator arranges for child care at each group meeting, finding an appropriate space for child care so parents and guardians may be close by, yet separated enough so children do not unnecessarily distract the group. A room next door or just across the hall is ideal. The child care coordinator should also ensure that an appropriately mature caregiver is on hand. The younger the children are, the more caregivers there should be. For example, the National Resource Center for Health and Safety in Child Care (http://nrc.uchsc.edu/) indicates that one caregiver should care for no more than three infants at one time.

REFRESHMENTS COORDINATOR

The refreshments coordinator arranges for coffee, juice, cookies, fruit, or other light snacks to be available at each group meeting. At the first session, the leader or refreshments coordinator will likely take responsibility for providing the items. Beyond the first group gathering, the refreshments coordinator can arrange for other members of the group to volunteer or take turns with this task. While the time of day will suggest the amount and type of refreshments offered, the refreshments coordinator should assist volunteers in providing a variety of refreshments that include healthy choices, such as fruits and fruit juices, in addition to more traditional options, such as coffee and cookies.

CLEAN-UP CREW COORDINATOR

The clean-up crew coordinator finds out how the meeting space should be arranged, learns where items are stored between sessions, and invites participants to be part of the clean-up crew. Members of the clean-up crew put away materials; pick up any plates, cups, or other refreshment items left behind; and do what is necessary to prepare the meeting space for its next use.

PARTICIPANT

Participants read the study material in advance of each meeting, make attendance at sessions a high priority, share ideas during the sessions, tolerate the opinions and ideas of others, and respond as they are able to requests of the leader and the various coordinators.

All members of the group may fulfill one or more of these roles at any time:
ENCOURAGER affirms others for the contributions they make to the discussion and invites others to speak. Encouragers help all group members participate and make their ideas heard.

SUMMARIZER pulls together main ideas from previous discussions. A summarizer briefly re-states the key ideas that have emerged in order to help the group stay focused and, when ready, move on to the next question or the next stage of conversation.

HARMONIZER helps group members accept differing ideas or conflicting beliefs. When group members disagree, a harmonizer helps others see what their ideas have in common and helps participants remember that full agreement is neither possible nor necessary.

GATE-KEEPER keeps members from dominating conversation and helps others join in. The gate-keeper watches for the person who wants to speak but can't get a word in and reminds vocal group members to listen for those who are less assertive.

INITIATOR contributes new thoughts or ideas, and is often the first to speak. An initiator gets things rolling by raising new questions or offering new insights that the rest of the group can talk about. The initiator is not always the leader, as others also will have new ideas.

INFORMER offers information from research or other sources. The informer keeps the conversation running by adding pertinent facts or observations from readings, personal knowledge, prior studies, or other sources.

CLARIFIER asks questions to help the group understand information or ideas more clearly. A clarifier understands that there are no stupid questions, and that assumptions can lead to misunderstandings.

INTERPRETER tries to restate the ideas of others in ways that can help the group better understand. An interpreter can step in when a group member is having trouble articulating an idea or is struggling to put things another way for others to understand.

TESTER asks questions to challenge current thinking and generate more discussion. Testing questions are not hostile or angry, but are designed to help group members think about things in a new way or from a different perspective.

STANDARD-SETTER reminds the group of its ground rules, when needed. By setting standards, this participant keeps the discussion on track.

COVENANT

We agree to join with others in this study and discussion group to open the Book of Faith together.

It is our understanding that . . .
* No prior knowledge of the Bible is expected or required.
* Members will not be forced to speak if we are not comfortable doing so.
* Group members are expected to respect each other's views.

We will do our best to . . .
* Read the study material in advance of each session.
* Make attendance at sessions a high priority.
* Share our ideas in the sessions, speaking as we are able.
* Tolerate the opinions and ideas of others.
* Keep personal things spoken in our time together confidential.
* Respond as we are able to requests of the leader and the various coordinators.
* Pray for the group gathered for study.

Signature _____ Date _____

Group Members   Phone/email
_____   _____

_____   _____

_____   _____

_____   _____

_____   _____

_____   _____

_____   _____

_____   _____

_____   _____

_____   _____

Rediscovering the Family Album of God's People

BIG IDEA

The stories and writings of the Old Testament developed as a witness to who God is.

IN THIS SESSION

The Old Testament is a witness to God's activity in the world. It's like a family album filled with stories about God and God's people that was passed from generation to generation. At first, stories were told orally, and later they were written down, with each generation adding its own stories along the way. Accounts of battles and blood, greed and power struggles, sin, sex, and pride. But the most important stories tell of the people's encounters with God. Because of these, this album has been kept and cherished through the centuries as canon, or sacred collection.

In this session you will:

✳ Get to know one another by learning names and backgrounds.

✳ See the Old Testament as the family album of the stories of God's people.

✳ Understand that the Old Testament has come to us through a long process.

GATHER 10 MINUTES

ICE-BREAKER: SPEED MEETING

If you brought a family photo album, scrapbook, or family Bible, great! Otherwise, search your billfold, cell phone, or PDA for a photo of yourself, your family, or someone special. If you don't have a photo, think of a favorite family memory. Get ready to quickly tell another person the story behind your photo or family memory. After pairing up with another participant, follow these steps:

1. Introduce yourself to your partner.
2. Tell your partner how long you've lived in this community and what brought you here.
3. Tell about your photo or memory, and listen as your partner tells you a story.
4. At your leader's signal, switch to the next partner and repeat the process at step 1.

Talk fast! Your leader will move you from partner to partner quickly so many in the group have a chance to get acquainted.

OPENING PRAYER

Gracious God, we thank you for the memories and stories we have to share. We thank you for the people and events that have shaped us. As we gather to rediscover our book of faith and the stories of your people of old, help us understand that these people and stories have helped make us who and what we are today. Open our eyes to your presence and your promises shown through the Bible. Amen.

✳ **STUDY** 30 MINUTES

As you watch chapter 1 of the DVD, use this space to take notes or write down questions.

THE ORAL TRADITION

The sun has just slipped behind the hills to the west, and the activity around the campsite is quieting. Most of the clan members have gathered around the fire. An old man walks on unsteady legs into the circle. As he sits, a hush falls over the gathering. The old man begins to sing:

> "Thus the LORD saved Israel that day from the Egyptians; and Israel saw the Egyptians dead on the seashore. Israel saw the great work that the LORD did against the Egyptians. So the people feared the LORD and believed in the LORD and in his servant Moses.
>
> Then Moses and the Israelites sang this song to the Lord: 'I will sing to the LORD, for he has triumphed gloriously;
>   horse and rider he has thrown into the sea.
> The LORD is my strength and my might,
>   and he has become my salvation.'"
> (Exodus 14:30–15:2a)

Before there were web pages or television, before magazines, books, paper, or pencils—before there was even an alphabet—there were songs and stories. The accounts were passed from one generation to the next. And because there were no written records, the stories were all people had to remember where they had come from and who they were. These songs and stories were of supreme importance. They were holy.

Here are some of the stories told by people living in the land that came to be called Israel. Mark the stories you know with an X.

- ☐ Adam and Eve in the Garden (Genesis 2–3)
- ☐ Noah and the flood (Genesis 6–9)
- ☐ Sarah and Abraham (Genesis 12–25)
- ☐ Joseph and his coat (Genesis 37–47)
- ☐ Moses and Pharaoh (Exodus 1–14)
- ☐ Crossing the Red Sea (Exodus 14–15)
- ☐ Joshua and the battle of Jericho (Joshua 1–6)
- ☐ Deborah and the battle at Mt. Tabor (Judges 4–5)

THE WRITTEN WORD

Storytellers who could remember and recite long stories had a unique talent. Usually, only a few people in each clan or tribe could master the art of storytelling. These few were very important people! They would perform stories on special occasions during the year.

The invention of writing meant the witness of God's people could be preserved in a new way for future generations. About the time Solomon was king of Israel and Judah (around 950—922 BC), the process of writing down oral stories began. People called scribes spent several years learning to read and write. They captured and reproduced the stories of God's people on scrolls—long strips of animal skins rolled on sticks—which were very durable. Over time, the account of God's people came to include stories, songs, prayers, laws, proverbs, and prophetic messages. In addition to recording the story of God's people, the scribes also read these witnesses aloud to the people at special times and places to help God's people rediscover who God is, much as the oral storytellers had done.

The Bible contains many kinds of writing. What types of literature do you read? Mark them with an "X." Next to each type, list the titles or genres you like to read.

☐ Newspapers _____

☐ Magazines _____

☐ Books (non-fiction) _____

☐ Books (fiction) _____

☐ Poetry _____

☐ Web sites _____

THE OLD TESTAMENT "CANON"

A *cannon* (with two *n*'s) is a very large gun, but a *canon* (with one *n*) is a collection—usually a collection of writings. As the stories of God's people were written down, there were debates about which scrolls to regard most highly. The debate was not about which stories were true records of the past, but about which had more authority for how people ought to live now. The scrolls considered most important were those that helped a new generation discover God.

All agreed that the witness collected in Genesis, Exodus, Leviticus, Numbers, and Deuteronomy—which is sometimes called the Torah or the Pentateuch—was the most important. A group known as the Sadducees included only these five books in their canon. Others, such as a group called the Pharisees, argued for a larger collection of books, including some that are not part of the canon for many Christians.

The Hebrew Bible, which Christians today call the Old Testament, is a collection of 39 different writings. The Old Testament includes the Pentateuch, plus words of prophets, Psalms, proverbs, and many stories about kings and queens, armies, spies, priests, and miracle workers. In all of it, God is the star. Our book of faith shows us who God is and how our faithful ancestors came to know God.

* Genesis   * Leviticus   * Judges
* Job   * Psalms   * Song of Solomon
* Jeremiah   * Daniel   * Malachi

Skim one (or more) of the Bible books listed above.
* How would you describe the type of material in this book?
* What is this book about?
* What does it say about God?
* At first glance, what books would you most want to read? Why?

✳ **SHARE** 15 MINUTES

The Old Testament is a collection of stories about the lives of God's people over many centuries. Some are the stories of great triumphs. Others tell of bitter defeats. As God's people reflected on these stories, they remembered how God had been present in good times and in bad. At the moment, it was not always clear that God was with them, but looking back, God's presence was clear.

God's presence is not always clear in our lives. But by looking to Scripture and looking back on our own experiences, we often become aware of how God has been with us through times of trial and times of joy. These stories become part of our personal family albums, as well.

Option 1—Letter to the Future

Write a letter to a future relative about an important story in your life where you know God was present. You could tell the story of your wedding day, a child's birth, a special trip or vacation, or another meaningful memory. Consider these questions as you write, and try to answer them in your letter:

✳ What's the story? What happened?

✳ Why is this event important to your life's story?

✳ Why do you want future generations to know about it?

✳ How was God present in this story?

✳ What hopes do you have for future generations?

Tuck the letter in an envelope, and consider adding other things that would help preserve the story, such as photos or other mementos.

Every life story has ups and downs. Create a life graph to record some high and low points in your life. What have been highlights over the last 5, 10, 15, and 20 years? When have you experienced low points? Track these on your graph, and then connect the points. Share your life graph with a partner and discuss these questions together.

✳ As you look back on the highs and lows of the last 20 years, where do you find evidence of God's presence?

✳ How would you have expected God to be present in these events?

✳ How might God have been acting through people's words, stories, or acts of kindness? Which can you recall?

✳ What do you hope for the next five years?

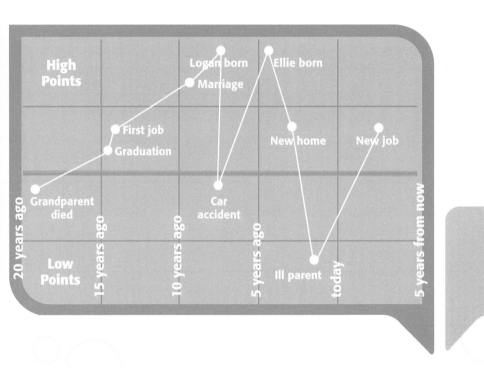

SEND 5 MINUTES

TAKE IT WITH YOU

Before you go, choose one of these options to do between now and the next session. Share your decision with at least one other person, and try to check in with that person in the coming week.

☐ **Option 1—Create a Family Album**

Start a family photo album, journal, or scrapbook to record your family's stories for future generations. Include at least one page about how faith in God impacts your lives.

☐ **Option 2—Rediscover the Book of Faith**

Block out about 15 minutes each day this week to spend time with the Bible. Pick one Old Testament book to focus on—perhaps Genesis, Exodus, Joshua, Judges, Ruth, Psalms, or Isaiah. Have paper or a notebook next to you as you read. Write down insights and questions that come up. Why do you think these stories are part of the Old Testament canon? Make plans to discuss your reflections with your pastor or another knowledgeable person.

☐ **Option 3—Record an Oral History**

Seek out your oldest living family member and conduct an oral history of your family. Use a tape recorder, mp3 recorder, video camera, or other device to preserve the interview. Ask the relative to share a family story. Perhaps it's a childhood tale, a story passed down from previous generations, or an account of life during times of depression, war, or prosperity. Be open to hearing more stories as the family member has energy to share.

☐ **Option 4—Discover Your Local Story**

Explore the history of your congregation. Locate histories written for church anniversaries or town centennials, or interview a long-time church member. How have people encountered God in your local area? Report back to the group in the next session.

CLOSING PRAYER

Gracious God, we thank you for the memories and stories we have to share. We thank you for the people and events that have shaped us. As we go our separate ways, help us to acknowledge the story we hold in common, the story of your love for your people in every time and every place. Give us courage to share this story with those we love and those we meet along our journey. Amen.

Rediscovering the Good News of Jesus

BIG IDEA

The New Testament records the struggle of the church to answer Jesus' question, "Who do you say that I am?"

IN THIS SESSION

Who was Jesus? Before there was a New Testament, there were communities of people who believed God had done something totally new—in and through Jesus—that transformed their lives. But God's startling act of raising Jesus from death also raised many questions in these communities: Who was Jesus? What did his resurrection really mean? This session looks at how the stories about Jesus gathered communities together. It also explores how, through their writings, early Christians shared their pictures of who Jesus was and is.

In this session you will:

* Learn how the early stories and words about Jesus formed a community.

* Understand that the letters of Paul, the Gospels, and Revelation were written for particular people at a particular time.

* Be able to describe how the collection of writings, later known as the New Testament, took shape.

GATHER 10 MINUTES

ICE-BREAKER: A MESSAGE FOR YOU

If you brought a special letter or email message to share, get it out. If not, think about a card, letter, or email that has been meaningful for you. Pair up with someone new, share your letter, and discuss a few of these questions together:

* What letter or note have you kept for a long time? Why?
* What does it feel like to get a letter or email from someone special?
* What kinds of correspondence do you save?
* Have you and another person ever aired disagreements through letters or email? What happened?
* Why do people write rather than simply call or wait until they can speak in person?

OPENING PRAYER

Gracious God, as you gathered the first believers into communities led by the Spirit, gather us now as a living community to share and understand your living Word. Be with us in our discussion and grant us insight. Touch our hearts and minds so we can see and feel your promises at work in our lives and our world. In Jesus' name, Amen.

✳ **STUDY** 30 MINUTES

As you watch chapter 2 of the DVD, use this space to take notes or write down questions.

WHO DO YOU SAY THAT I AM?

> Now when Jesus came into the district of Caesarea Philippi, he asked his disciples, "Who do people say that the Son of Man is?" And they said, "Some say John the Baptist, but others Elijah, and still others Jeremiah or one of the prophets." He said to them, "But who do you say that I am?" Simon Peter answered, "You are the Messiah, the Son of the living God. (Matthew 16:13-16)

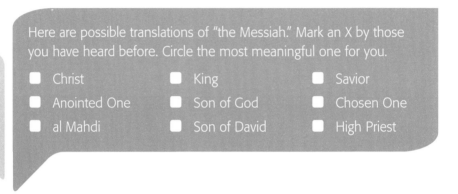

Here are possible translations of "the Messiah." Mark an X by those you have heard before. Circle the most meaningful one for you.

- ☐ Christ
- ☐ King
- ☐ Savior
- ☐ Anointed One
- ☐ Son of God
- ☐ Chosen One
- ☐ al Mahdi
- ☐ Son of David
- ☐ High Priest

Jesus of Nazareth was executed by Roman authorities outside the Jewish city of Jerusalem sometime around the year 30 A.D. He was killed on a cross, which suggests that the Romans considered him a criminal. Jesus claimed to be "King of the Jews," and Caesar couldn't allow rival kings. The execution was successful. It must have seemed to Jesus' followers that the death of Jesus was the end, just as the Romans intended.

But an amazing thing happened. Women from the burial committee discovered that Jesus was not dead, but alive! Jesus was resurrected. Transformed. This was something totally new! Jesus' followers praised the God "who raised Jesus from the dead." Jesus was a king—but unlike any king the world had ever known. The early followers had to tell that news.

The movement quickly grew from a tiny group near Jerusalem to many throughout the Eastern Mediterranean. Imagine the questions when someone announced that "God raised Jesus from the dead." Who is Jesus? What God? Why was Jesus dead? What difference does it make? Before early Christian writings, Jesus' followers told stories, sang hymns, and shared their experiences in order to answer these questions.

LETTERS, GOSPELS, AND APOCALYPSE

The early believers already had the religious texts of ancient Israel. They included the stories of Genesis, the Exodus, and Israel's kings. The texts also contained the words of Israel's prophets and the poetry of Israel's Psalms. Jesus' followers believed that the God who spoke to Abraham and Moses had also raised Jesus from the dead. The New Testament writings we have today grew out of the church's storytelling, preaching, and worship. These writings were put down on parchment over a period of almost one hundred years, and three main kinds of literature emerged.

Letters: Through these writings, Jesus' followers encouraged and taught one another. The apostle Paul wrote many of the letters that appear in the New Testament. He gathered communities, most of them Gentiles (non-Jews) who believed in the risen Lord. As these communities wrestled with what Jesus meant for their lives and their world, Paul offered practical advice through his letters. Paul answered their questions about marriage, circumcision, and what they should or should not eat.

Gospels: These writings shared the news of grace and salvation through Jesus' death and resurrection. Although they appear first in our New Testament, the Gospels were actually written after most of the letters. They are not really histories or biographies, but a special kind of literature designed to answer the question, "Who do you say that I am?" The first three Gospels in our Bible (Matthew, Mark, and Luke) contain many of the same stories and patterns. The Gospel of John has many stories not found in the other Gospels.

Revelation: Revelation is an apocalyptic letter written in a very different style than most Bible texts. Through rich imagery, Revelation offers advice to churches that were facing persecution for their faith. The style may be strange to us today, but it was very familiar at the time.

Form three groups to investigate the main types of writing in the New Testament. Then put together a one-minute presentation to share what you discovered with the rest of the group. Be creative!

Group 1: Letters	Group 2: Gospels	Group 3: Apocalypse
Thessalonians 4:13-18 is an answer to a question that believers in Thessalonica asked Paul. This biblical letter contains Paul's answer.	Compare how one Gospel begins and ends. Look at the first chapter and answer the question: Who is Jesus in this passage? Then ask the same question after reading the crucifixion scene (Matthew 27:32-55; Mark 15:21-39; Luke 23:32-47; or John 19:16-30).	Look at the stanzas of the "Battle Hymn of the Republic" (*Evangelical Lutheran Worship* 890). Then read Revelation 14:14-20; 19:11-21; and 21:1-27.
✱ What do you think the question was? ✱ What was Paul's answer? ✱ What kinds of questions do Christians ask today?	✱ What do you think is the most important part of this Gospel's crucifixion account?	✱ How do you feel as you read the hymn and these passages? ✱ Who do they say Jesus is?

LOOSE CANONS

The early Christian communities started sharing letters and Gospels because these writings were helpful, useful, and faith-building. The earliest collections may have been a few of Paul's letters. For example, 1 and 2 Corinthians, Galatians, and Romans captured some essential statements about who Jesus is. They also touched on questions many communities were struggling with: When will Jesus return? How do we live in the time while we wait? How do we relate to the world around us?

By the second century, the Christian movement expanded, and more non-Jews became believers. Many Christian writings circulated among the early churches. Deciding on a canon was not an easy or quick process. Some people, such as Marcion and Tatian, developed their own canons, including the writings they considered to be Holy Scripture. This only pressed the debate further: Which writings were truly inspired by the Holy Spirit? Should the Hebrew Bible be kept with the new writings produced by the Christian communities? What new writings should be included?

Eventually, three key criteria surfaced:

1. Who was the author? Was the writing associated with one of the apostles? (Apostolicity)
2. How well did the writing reflect the community's beliefs about who Jesus was and is? (Orthodoxy)
3. Was the writing commonly used and well-known to the Christian churches? (Universality)

Through years of discussion, prayer, and the Holy Spirit's guidance and inspiration, the community narrowed down what we call the New Testament to 27 writings.

Christians today still wrestle with how the Holy Scriptures inform our lives and our responses to important questions. Add to this list of the Christian community's questions and debates from the past and present.

* Circumcision
* Dietary Laws
* Climate Change
* Faith and Politics

The resurrection of Jesus was a shocking, amazing, bewildering event. For many decades, early Christians debated, preached, sang, and wrote to one another about what it meant. Through this long give-and-take, Christians were invited to consider for themselves the answer to Jesus' question in Matthew 16, "Who do you say that I am?"

The New Testament challenges us to struggle with that question today. Not everyone will arrive at the same answer. But those who answer, with Peter, "You are the Messiah," are called into the community that is the church. Even if we do not agree on all of the details in the answers to our questions about Jesus, the church is the place where we gather together with those who are asking the same questions.

Option 1—Personal Canon

Most of us have a "personal canon." This personal canon may include certain Bible passages, hymns, and songs that help us express and share our faith and answer the question of who Jesus is. What is your personal canon? What sources do you turn to when you need inspiration, feel down, or have questions about your faith?

Share your personal canon with two or three others in the group. Listen as they share their personal canons, as well. What, if any, "writings" do you have in common? Why do these hold so much meaning for you?

> What is your personal canon? What sources do you turn to when you need inspiration, feel down, or have questions about your faith?

Option 2—Picturing Jesus

Look at artists' depictions of Jesus. In pairs or trios, study one of the images in depth, discussing how it portrays who Jesus is.

Use these questions to guide your conversation.

* What key elements are depicted?
* Why might the artist have highlighted these points?
* What does this image say about Jesus? What story does it tell?
* How is this similar to or different from my understanding of who Jesus is?

Pair up with another group and share your reflections with each other. Together, think about the fact that no photos or paintings exist from when Jesus was on earth—all have been imagined by artists years later. Why do you think artists and other believers have tried to "put a face on Jesus"?

TAKE IT WITH YOU

Before you go, choose one of these options to do between now and the next session. Share your decision with at least one other person and try to check in with that person in the coming week.

☐ Option 1—It's Ornamental

Pull out some of your Christmas ornaments and look at them closely. How do the decorations reflect New Testament stories? Do these decorations help bring the story to life? How do these decorations answer Jesus' question, "Who do you say that I am?" If you find one ornament that is particularly meaningful, hang it somewhere in your home.

☐ Option 2—Movie Night

Watch a film about Jesus. *Jesus Christ Superstar, Godspell, The Passion of the Christ,* and *The Greatest Story Ever Told* have all been popular, and each has a different perspective on the Gospel story. As you watch, think about how the film answers Jesus' question, "Who do you say that I am?" How does it compare to how you would answer that question?

☐ Option 3—My Music

There are many songs about Jesus and who Jesus is in popular music as well as sacred music. Reflect on a popular song or favorite hymn that talks about Jesus. Begin a personal collection of music that best answers the question, "Who do you say Jesus is?"

☐ Option 4 – Catechism

Find a copy of *The Small Catechism* by Martin Luther. Look at Luther's explanations for the second and third articles of the Creed and the petitions of the Lord's Prayer. What answer does Luther put forward to the question, "Who do you say that I am?"

CLOSING PRAYER

Leader: *The Lord be with you.*

Participants: *And also with you.*

L: *On the cross Jesus prayed for us,*

P: **Empower us to pray for others.**

L: *We are all learning about God's Word.*

P: **We also need to learn how to pray.**

L: *Let us pray the words Jesus taught us, as witnessed in the Gospel of Luke:*

All: **Father, hallowed be your name. Your kingdom come. Give us each day our daily bread. And forgive us our sins, for we ourselves forgive everyone indebted to us. And do not bring us to the time of trial. Amen.** *(Luke 11:2-4)*

Rediscovering God's Gift of Grace

BIG IDEA

When Martin Luther sparked the Reformation, the Christian community rediscovered the Bible as a book of faith.

IN THIS SESSION

The Bible has not always been widely available to Christians; prior to Martin Luther's time, it was only printed in its original languages of Hebrew and Greek or the scholarly language of Latin. Luther was among the first to translate the Bible into the common language of the people. His translation came at a time when the printing press was a new and revolutionary technology, enabling the Bible to be mass-produced and purchased more cheaply. As a result, God's Word became available to more people than ever, and God's Spirit used this availability to change the face of the Christian church.

In this session you will:

✳ Describe how Luther's translation of the Bible made it accessible to anyone instead of just clergy.

✳ Understand how the printing press made the Bible available and affordable in new ways.

✳ Understand how the Reformation transformed the ways Christians today understand and interpret Scripture.

GATHER 10 MINUTES

ICEBREAKER: MIX AND MINGLE

Think of your own answer for each of the following questions. If you brought a type of technology with you, great! If not, think of one you use regularly and appreciate.

* How many languages can you speak?
* When did you last buy a book?
* What is your favorite form of technology?

Starting with the first question, mingle with the group and find out other members' answers. When you find someone who has a similar answer as you do, stay with them. Together, continue mingling, sticking with people who have similar answers. As your leader directs, repeat the ice-breaker for the remaining questions.

OPENING PRAYER

Mighty God, you are bigger than we could ever imagine. We stand in awe of your grace and mercy and praise you for your power and goodness. Be with us as we explore your Word and what it means for our lives today. Amen.

✳ STUDY 30 MINUTES

As you watch chapter 3 of the DVD, use this space to take notes or write down questions.

In all his life, Dietrich never understood the language of worship because it was written and said in Latin. He understood the sermons though; the priests preached in his native tongue, German. They warned him of the reasons he might go to purgatory to work off a lifetime of sins before entering heaven. His faith was one of fear, of trying to "earn" salvation.

Now, his faith was turning from fear to anger. His beloved little girl Anna had died a year before. Every time the priest spoke of Christ's judgment, Dietrich cringed, imagining his poor daughter suffering in purgatory.

Then, Johann Tetzel came to his village and offered a way to override God's judgment. Tetzel told the people about certificates of indulgence. Once purchased, the certificate promised the immediate passage of a dead loved one from purgatory and into heaven's gates. It was far too expensive for Dietrich, but how could he put a price on his daughter's soul?

One reason legalism and abuses (such as indulgences) were common in the medieval church was because the Bible was not easily accessible to everyday people. Instead, people relied on the church to convey the Bible's message. But the message of salvation through Jesus Christ on the cross became overshadowed as some leaders gave into greed and corruption.

> What keeps Christians from reading the Bible today? Begin with these reasons, and add others you can think of. Circle the ones that resonate with you.
>
> Too busy   Not relevant
>
> Difficult to understand   Controversies
>
> Not interesting

GO GUTENBERG

There was a day when every Bible that existed had been painstakingly written by hand. Because books were so difficult and time-consuming to produce, they were very expensive. Cost wasn't the only factor keeping the Bible out of reach. Bibles were written in Hebrew, Greek, and Latin—languages of scholars. Therefore, owning a Bible was a rare luxury.

As Luther studied Scripture, he discovered we are saved by Christ's work alone. Along with passages in Romans, Galatians, and Hebrews, Ephesians 2:8 captures this realization: "For by grace you have been saved through faith, and this is not your own doing; it is the gift of God."

Luther's spiritual awakening came at the perfect time. Luther sat at his desk at Wartburg Castle, feverishly translating the New Testament from its original Greek into German. A month later, this so-called *September Testament* was complete. Meanwhile, Johann Gutenberg's marvelous new invention, the printing press, was producing books at an unimaginable speed.

Thousands of copies of Luther's "common language" Bible as well as other theological writings went from the printing press into the hands of spiritually hungry people. Without this technology, the Reformation would have taken many years, perhaps decades, to flourish.

Discuss these questions in groups of two or three.

* Why do you think the Luther's translation of the New Testament became a bestseller so quickly? What did it offer?
* Besides reading it yourself, how do you hear God's word?
* How do the modern-day communication technologies make the Bible more readily available? (Consider radio, Internet, CDs, DVDs, televisions, mp3 players, cell phones, etc.)
* What limits do these technologies have when it comes to portraying the Bible?

THIS IS YOUR BRAIN ON GOSPEL

Over the course of his study and writings, Martin Luther recognized that the Bible speaks with two voices—law and gospel. The voice of the law requires action and perfection from us. It points out our brokenness and sin; it condemns us. With its gospel voice, the Bible proclaims that Christ has set us free from the law and made us God's children.

This is your brain as the law does its work.

> *Aw geez. What was I thinking? I shouldn't have even stopped at the candy machine when I saw those two standing next to it. I knew they'd be whispering about Carl and Sally; I knew they'd ask me for details. Once I started talking, I couldn't stop. Shut up! I should have stayed away, but every piece of chocolate in the vending machine was screaming for me to eat it. I'm rotten. Now I've gone and fed the gossip. I fed my thighs with chocolate, too. Goodbye, diet number 26. I'm so weak. Rotten and weak. I need another candy bar. Or maybe a cupcake. Ooh! How about both? Man, I'm going to Hell.*

This is your brain as the gospel does its work (the following Sunday, on your way back to your seat after communion).

> *Mmm. Should communion bread taste that good? Why not? For me, huh? Given for me. Christ is here for me. Cool. Hey, there's Sally and Carl—they're such a cute couple. I'm so happy they found each other. God has really blessed them. And God has blessed me so much, every single day. I can't believe Jesus loves me enough to die on the cross for my sins. For all of us, so we might live. Wow, that makes me really want to share that love with others. I think I'll invite Sally and Carl over for dinner. Man, God rocks!*

As we read scripture, we can hear both law and gospel. Read each passage. On the spectrum, indicate if the verse seems more like law or gospel to you.

1. By grace you have been saved through faith. (Ephesians 2:8)

   Law ●————————————————————————● Gospel

2. All have sinned and fall short of the glory of God. (Romans 3:23)

   Law ●————————————————————————● Gospel

3. I will be with you; I will not fail you or forsake you. (Joshua 1:5)

   Law ●————————————————————————● Gospel

4. You shall love your neighbor as yourself. (Mark 12:31)

   Law ●————————————————————————● Gospel

5. God is our refuge and strength. (Psalm 46:1)

   Law ●————————————————————————● Gospel

6. It will be hard for a rich person to enter the kingdom of heaven. (Matthew 19:23)

   Law ●————————————————————————● Gospel

7. This is my body, which is given for you. Do this in remembrance of me. (Luke 22:19)

   Law ●————————————————————————● Gospel

8. Honor your father and your mother. (Exodus 20:12)

   Law ●————————————————————————● Gospel

9. For my thoughts are not your thoughts, nor are your ways my ways, says the LORD. (Isaiah 55:8)

   Law ●————————————————————————● Gospel

10. So faith by itself, if it has no works, is dead. (James 2:17)

    Law ●————————————————————————● Gospel

Compare your marks with another person. Where are they similar? Where did you interpret the phrase differently? Why might it be helpful to look for both law and gospel when reading the Bible?

Luther's Bible translation, its rapid publication, and the Reformation transformed faith communities. By getting the Bible into the hands of the people, the Christian community rediscovered a grace-filled faith in Jesus that has reshaped the world.

Even today the people of God wrestle with how to understand and interpret Scripture. We face challenges as we try to live in tension between the law and the gospel. Thankfully, God is still at work among us. Several hundred years later, we are still part of a reforming church.

Option 1—One Word, Many Translations

When Luther translated the Bible into German, it meant the community of believers could access the Scriptures in new ways. Christians today don't face the same struggle as people in Luther's day. Not only has the Bible been printed in hundreds of languages, but there are many versions in English alone.

It can still be challenging to find a Bible that makes it easy for you to be in God's Word daily so the Bible can inform your faith. In groups of three or four, create a list of criteria you'd look for in a Bible. Then review some of the Bible translations provided by your leader. Which ones would open up Scripture to you most? Share your thoughts with the rest of the group.

Criteria I look for in a Bible

Option 2—Grace Notes

Luther's rediscovery of God's grace and forgiveness was a major reason he worked so hard to spread the good news of the power of Christ's death and resurrection. He wanted to share this understanding so others could rediscover who God is and what that meant for their lives.

Take the opportunity to share the promise of God's grace with someone else. Write a card or letter to a person you know who could use encouragement. You may even want to include the promise of Ephesians 2:8: "For by grace you have been saved through faith, and this is not your own doing; it is the gift of God." Mail or give the note to the person the next time you meet.

SEND 5 MINUTES

TAKE IT WITH YOU

Before you go, choose one of these options to do between now and the next session. Share your decision with at least one other person and try to check in with that person in the coming week.

Option 1—The Big Picture

One reason Luther translated the Bible was so people would have access to *all* of God's Word. In worship, we hear parts of the Bible but don't always get the big picture. Over the next week, try to read one Gospel entirely. (Tip: Mark is the shortest Gospel.) Keep a notebook nearby and write down ideas or questions that come up. How does reading one book in depth over a short time period change how you understand it?

Option 2—Word in Worship

Volunteer to read the Bible passage for a worship service at your church. To prepare, read your passage through silently a few times. Where do you hear law and gospel in the text? Practice reading the passage aloud in different tones, cadences, and inflections to see what makes the text come alive.

Option 3—A Reformed World

Investigate Luther's world and how the Reformation transformed the church. Pick one topic to learn more about—such as what Luther's life was like as a monk, what Luther said in the Ninety-Five Theses about the church's abuse of power, or another subject of interest. Then research your topic on the Internet, at the library, or during a conversation with a pastor or confirmation leader.

Option 4—Changed Perspectives

Choose one of your favorite Bible passages or stories—perhaps one that has changed or influenced how you understand God. Create a piece of art that portrays this Bible text. Use any medium you like, such as paint, collage, jewelry, sculpture, or photography. Put it in a place where you will see it often.

CLOSING PRAYER

Wonderful God, We praise you for this day.
God's Word is at work.

Thank you for your glorious creation.
God's Word is at work.

Thank you for the gift of forgiveness.
God's Word is at work.

Thank you for the gift of faith.
God's Word is at work.

Most of all, we thank you for the living Word, your Son Jesus Christ our Lord. Amen.

(Adapted from 1 Thessalonians 2:13)